AF454239

Baby Shower For

Date

Copyright © 2020 by Luis Lukesun
All rights reserved.  No part of this book may be reproduced without written permission of the copyright owner, except for the use of limited quotations for the purpose of book reviews.

Guest Name

Relationship to Parents

Advice for Parents

Wishes for Baby

Guest Name

Relationship to Parents

Advice for Parents

Wishes for Baby

Guest Name

Relationship to Parents

Advice for Parents

Wishes for Baby

Guest Name

Relationship to Parents

Advice for Parents

Wishes for Baby

Guest Name

Relationship to Parents

Advice for Parents

Wishes for Baby

Guest Name

Relationship to Parents

Advice for Parents

Wishes for Baby

Guest Name

Relationship to Parents

Advice for Parents

Wishes for Baby

Guest Name

Relationship to Parents

Advice for Parents

Wishes for Baby

Guest Name

Relationship to Parents

Advice for Parents

Wishes for Baby

Guest Name

Relationship to Parents

Advice for Parents

Wishes for Baby

Guest Name

Relationship to Parents

Advice for Parents

Wishes for Baby

Guest Name

Relationship to Parents

Advice for Parents

Wishes for Baby

Guest Name

Relationship to Parents

Advice for Parents

Wishes for Baby

Guest Name

Relationship to Parents

Advice for Parents

Wishes for Baby

Guest Name

Relationship to Parents

Advice for Parents

Wishes for Baby

Guest Name

Relationship to Parents

Advice for Parents

Wishes for Baby

Guest Name

_______________________________________________

Relationship to Parents

_______________________________________________

Advice for Parents

_______________________________________________

_______________________________________________

_______________________________________________

_______________________________________________

Wishes for Baby

_______________________________________________

_______________________________________________

_______________________________________________

_______________________________________________

Guest Name

_______________________________________

Relationship to Parents

_______________________________________

Advice for Parents

_______________________________________

_______________________________________

_______________________________________

_______________________________________

Wishes for Baby

_______________________________________

_______________________________________

_______________________________________

Guest Name

_______________________________________

Relationship to Parents

_______________________________________

Advice for Parents

_______________________________________

_______________________________________

_______________________________________

Wishes for Baby

_______________________________________

_______________________________________

_______________________________________

Guest Name

Relationship to Parents

Advice for Parents

Wishes for Baby

Guest Name

Relationship to Parents

Advice for Parents

Wishes for Baby

Guest Name

Relationship to Parents

Advice for Parents

Wishes for Baby

Guest Name

Relationship to Parents

Advice for Parents

Wishes for Baby

Guest Name

Relationship to Parents

Advice for Parents

Wishes for Baby

Guest Name

Relationship to Parents

Advice for Parents

Wishes for Baby

Guest Name

Relationship to Parents

Advice for Parents

Wishes for Baby

Guest Name

Relationship to Parents

Advice for Parents

Wishes for Baby

Guest Name

Relationship to Parents

Advice for Parents

Wishes for Baby

Guest Name

Relationship to Parents

Advice for Parents

Wishes for Baby

Guest Name

Relationship to Parents

Advice for Parents

Wishes for Baby

Guest Name

Relationship to Parents

Advice for Parents

Wishes for Baby

Guest Name

_______________________________________

Relationship to Parents

_______________________________________

Advice for Parents

_______________________________________

_______________________________________

_______________________________________

Wishes for Baby

_______________________________________

_______________________________________

_______________________________________

Guest Name

Relationship to Parents

Advice for Parents

Wishes for Baby

Guest Name

Relationship to Parents

Advice for Parents

Wishes for Baby

Guest Name

_______________________________

Relationship to Parents

_______________________________

Advice for Parents

_______________________________

_______________________________

_______________________________

Wishes for Baby

_______________________________

_______________________________

_______________________________

Guest Name

Relationship to Parents

Advice for Parents

Wishes for Baby

Guest Name

Relationship to Parents

Advice for Parents

Wishes for Baby

Guest Name

Relationship to Parents

Advice for Parents

Wishes for Baby

Guest Name

_______________________________________

Relationship to Parents

_______________________________________

Advice for Parents

_______________________________________

_______________________________________

_______________________________________

Wishes for Baby

_______________________________________

_______________________________________

_______________________________________

Guest Name

Relationship to Parents

Advice for Parents

Wishes for Baby

Guest Name

Relationship to Parents

Advice for Parents

Wishes for Baby

Guest Name

Relationship to Parents

Advice for Parents

Wishes for Baby

Guest Name

Relationship to Parents

Advice for Parents

Wishes for Baby

Guest Name

Relationship to Parents

Advice for Parents

Wishes for Baby

Guest Name

_______________________________________

Relationship to Parents

_______________________________________

Advice for Parents

_______________________________________

_______________________________________

_______________________________________

_______________________________________

Wishes for Baby

_______________________________________

_______________________________________

_______________________________________

Guest Name

_______________________________________________

Relationship to Parents

_______________________________________________

Advice for Parents

_______________________________________________

_______________________________________________

_______________________________________________

Wishes for Baby

_______________________________________________

_______________________________________________

_______________________________________________

Guest Name

Relationship to Parents

Advice for Parents

Wishes for Baby

Guest Name

Relationship to Parents

Advice for Parents

Wishes for Baby

Guest Name

Relationship to Parents

Advice for Parents

Wishes for Baby

Guest Name

Relationship to Parents

Advice for Parents

Wishes for Baby

Guest Name

Relationship to Parents

Advice for Parents

Wishes for Baby

Guest Name

Relationship to Parents

Advice for Parents

Wishes for Baby

Guest Name

Relationship to Parents

Advice for Parents

Wishes for Baby

Guest Name

Relationship to Parents

Advice for Parents

Wishes for Baby

Guest Name

Relationship to Parents

Advice for Parents

Wishes for Baby

Guest Name

Relationship to Parents

Advice for Parents

Wishes for Baby

Guest Name

Relationship to Parents

Advice for Parents

Wishes for Baby

Guest Name

Relationship to Parents

Advice for Parents

Wishes for Baby

Guest Name

Relationship to Parents

Advice for Parents

Wishes for Baby

Guest Name

Relationship to Parents

Advice for Parents

Wishes for Baby

Guest Name

_______________________________________________

Relationship to Parents

_______________________________________________

Advice for Parents

_______________________________________________

_______________________________________________

_______________________________________________

Wishes for Baby

_______________________________________________

_______________________________________________

_______________________________________________

Guest Name

Relationship to Parents

Advice for Parents

Wishes for Baby

Guest Name

_______________________________

Relationship to Parents

_______________________________

Advice for Parents

_______________________________

_______________________________

_______________________________

_______________________________

Wishes for Baby

_______________________________

_______________________________

_______________________________

Guest Name

Relationship to Parents

Advice for Parents

Wishes for Baby

Guest Name

Relationship to Parents

Advice for Parents

Wishes for Baby

Guest Name

Relationship to Parents

Advice for Parents

Wishes for Baby

Guest Name

Relationship to Parents

Advice for Parents

Wishes for Baby

Guest Name

_______________________________

Relationship to Parents

_______________________________

Advice for Parents

_______________________________

_______________________________

_______________________________

_______________________________

Wishes for Baby

_______________________________

_______________________________

_______________________________

Guest Name

Relationship to Parents

Advice for Parents

Wishes for Baby

Guest Name

Relationship to Parents

Advice for Parents

Wishes for Baby

Guest Name

Relationship to Parents

Advice for Parents

Wishes for Baby

Guest Name

_______________________________________________

Relationship to Parents

_______________________________________________

Advice for Parents

_______________________________________________

_______________________________________________

_______________________________________________

_______________________________________________

Wishes for Baby

_______________________________________________

_______________________________________________

_______________________________________________

_______________________________________________

Guest Name

Relationship to Parents

Advice for Parents

Wishes for Baby

Guest Name

Relationship to Parents

Advice for Parents

Wishes for Baby

Guest Name

_______________________________

Relationship to Parents

_______________________________

Advice for Parents

_______________________________

_______________________________

_______________________________

Wishes for Baby

_______________________________

_______________________________

_______________________________

_______________________________

Guest Name

Relationship to Parents

Advice for Parents

Wishes for Baby

Guest Name

Relationship to Parents

Advice for Parents

Wishes for Baby

Guest Name

Relationship to Parents

Advice for Parents

Wishes for Baby

Guest Name

Relationship to Parents

Advice for Parents

Wishes for Baby

Guest Name

Relationship to Parents

Advice for Parents

Wishes for Baby

Guest Name

Relationship to Parents

Advice for Parents

Wishes for Baby

Guest Name

Relationship to Parents

Advice for Parents

Wishes for Baby

Guest Name

_______________________________________

Relationship to Parents

_______________________________________

Advice for Parents

_______________________________________

_______________________________________

_______________________________________

Wishes for Baby

_______________________________________

_______________________________________

_______________________________________

Guest Name

Relationship to Parents

Advice for Parents

Wishes for Baby

Guest Name

Relationship to Parents

Advice for Parents

Wishes for Baby

Guest Name

Relationship to Parents

Advice for Parents

Wishes for Baby

Guest Name

Relationship to Parents

Advice for Parents

Wishes for Baby

Guest Name

Relationship to Parents

Advice for Parents

Wishes for Baby

Guest Name

Relationship to Parents

Advice for Parents

Wishes for Baby

Guest Name

Relationship to Parents

Advice for Parents

Wishes for Baby

Guest Name

Relationship to Parents

Advice for Parents

Wishes for Baby

Guest Name

Relationship to Parents

Advice for Parents

Wishes for Baby

Guest Name

Relationship to Parents

Advice for Parents

Wishes for Baby

Guest Name

_______________________________

Relationship to Parents

_______________________________

Advice for Parents

_______________________________

_______________________________

_______________________________

_______________________________

Wishes for Baby

_______________________________

_______________________________

_______________________________

Guest Name

Relationship to Parents

Advice for Parents

Wishes for Baby

Guest Name

Relationship to Parents

Advice for Parents

Wishes for Baby

Guest Name

Relationship to Parents

Advice for Parents

Wishes for Baby

Guest Name

Relationship to Parents

Advice for Parents

Wishes for Baby

Guest Name

Relationship to Parents

Advice for Parents

Wishes for Baby

Guest Name

Relationship to Parents

Advice for Parents

Wishes for Baby

# Notes / Photos

# Notes / Photos

# Notes / Photos

# Notes / Photos

# Notes / Photos

# Notes / Photos

# Notes / Photos

# Gift Log

| Name/Email/Phone | Gift |
|---|---|
| | |
| | |
| | |
| | |
| | |
| | |
| | |
| | |
| | |
| | |
| | |

# Gift Log

Name/Email/Phone   Gift

# Gift Log

Name/Email/Phone                    Gift

# Gift Log

Name/Email/Phone        Gift

# Gift Log

Name/Email/Phone | Gift

# Gift Log

| Name/Email/Phone | Gift |
| --- | --- |

# Gift Log

Name/Email/Phone                    Gift

# Gift Log

| Name/Email/Phone | Gift |
| --- | --- |

# Gift Log

| Name/Email/Phone | Gift |
| --- | --- |

# Gift Log

| Name/Email/Phone | Gift |
| --- | --- |
|  |  |